This book belongs to:

_____

Copyright 2019 ©

All rights reserved. No part of this publication may be copied, reproduced in any format, by any means, electronic or otherwise, without prior consent from the copywrite owner and publisher of this book.

How to use this Prayer Journal

This is a 60-day prayer journal and can be utilized to explore God's word surrounding different aspects of your life.

How to enjoy the book, Step by Step:

- You will find a list of subjects and corresponding Bible verses on the next page (page 3).

- Each day, select a verse.

- Place a check mark in the circle next to the verse you select indicating that you have completed your studies of the verse

- You will find a space at the top of each day's page to write in the verse that you selected for that day.

- Follow the prompts provided.

LONELINESS
- Psalm 25:16
- Matthew 28:20
- Isaiah 41:10
- 1 Peter 5:7
- Psalm 147:3
- John 16:32-33
- John 15:15

STRESS
- Psalm 46:1-3
- Philippians 4:6
- John 14:27
- Psalm 94:19
- Luke 12:25-26
- John 14:27
- Joshua 1:9

HEALTH
- Proverbs 17:22
- Jeremiah 33:6
- Proverbs 16:24
- Proverbs 3:7-8
- Jeremiah 17:14
- Exodus 23:25
- Isaiah 41:10

STUDENTS
- Matthew 11:28
- Hebrews 10:35-36
- Proverbs 3:5-6
- Psalm 27:14
- Joshua 1:9
- James 1:5-6
- 2 Corinthians 9:8

FINANCES
- Hebrews 13:5
- Matthew 6:21
- Psalm 37:16-17
- Proverbs 13:11
- Matthew 19:21
- Matthew 6:24
- 1 Timothy 6:10

MOTIVATION
- Colossians 3:23
- Matthew 19:26
- Philippians 4:19
- Philippians 4:13
- Jeremiah 29:11
- Romans 8:28
- John 10:10

DATING
- Ephesians 4:2-3
- 2 Corinthians 6:14
- Genesis 2:18
- 1 Corinthians 6:18
- Matthew 6:33
- 1 Corinthians 15:33

SLEEP
- Proverbs 3:24
- Psalm 3:5
- Psalm 4:8
- Psalm 127:2
- Exodus 33:14
- Psalm 13:3

MANAGE TIME
- Colossians 4:5
- Ephesians 5:15-17
- Jeremiah 29:11
- John 9:4
- Proverbs 16:9
- Ecclesiastes 3:1-8

Today's Date:_____

Let God speak to you through his Word. Select a scripture from Page 3.

Scripture selected:_____

Write down the scripture:

Study the scripture, then pray and answer the following.

Write down how you're feeling about the topic of the scripture:

_____

_____

_____

_____

What's your prayer to God surrounding the scripture?

_____

_____

_____

_____

Other Prayer Requests:

_____   _____
_____   _____
_____   _____
_____   _____

Answered Prayer Requests:

_____   _____
_____   _____
_____   _____
_____   _____

Today I am most thankful for:

_____
_____
_____
_____

Today's Date:_____

Let God speak to you through his Word. Select a scripture from Page 3.

Scripture selected:_____

Write down the scripture:

Study the scripture, then pray and answer the following.

Write down how you're feeling about the topic of the scripture:

_____

_____

_____

_____

What's your prayer to God surrounding the scripture?

_____

_____

_____

_____

Other Prayer Requests:

_____ _____

_____ _____

_____ _____

_____ _____

Answered Prayer Requests:

_____ _____

_____ _____

_____ _____

_____ _____

Today I am most thankful for:

_____

_____

_____

_____

Today's Date:_____

Let God speak to you through his Word. Select a scripture from Page 3.

Scripture selected:_____

Write down the scripture:

Study the scripture, then pray and answer the following.

Write down how you're feeling about the topic of the scripture:

_____
_____
_____
_____

What's your prayer to God surrounding the scripture?

_____
_____
_____
_____

Other Prayer Requests:

_____   _____
_____   _____
_____   _____
_____   _____

Answered Prayer Requests:

_____   _____
_____   _____
_____   _____
_____   _____

Today I am most thankful for:

_____
_____
_____
_____

Today's Date:_____

Let God speak to you through his Word. Select a scripture from Page 3.

Scripture selected:_____

Write down the scripture:

Study the scripture, then pray and answer the following.

Write down how you're feeling about the topic of the scripture:

_____
_____
_____
_____

What's your prayer to God surrounding the scripture?

_____
_____
_____
_____

Other Prayer Requests:

_____   _____
_____   _____
_____   _____
_____   _____

Answered Prayer Requests:

_____   _____
_____   _____
_____   _____
_____   _____

Today I am most thankful for:

_____
_____
_____
_____

Today's Date:_____

Let God speak to you through his Word. Select a scripture from Page 3.

Scripture selected:_____

Write down the scripture:

Study the scripture, then pray and answer the following.

Write down how you're feeling about the topic of the scripture:

_____

_____

_____

_____

What's your prayer to God surrounding the scripture?

_____

_____

_____

_____

Other Prayer Requests:

_____   _____

_____   _____

_____   _____

_____   _____

Answered Prayer Requests:

_____   _____

_____   _____

_____   _____

_____   _____

Today I am most thankful for:

_____

_____

_____

_____

Today's Date:_____

Let God speak to you through his Word. Select a scripture from Page 3.

Scripture selected:_____

Write down the scripture:

Study the scripture, then pray and answer the following.

Write down how you're feeling about the topic of the scripture:

_____
_____
_____
_____

What's your prayer to God surrounding the scripture?

_____
_____
_____
_____

Other Prayer Requests:

Answered Prayer Requests:

Today I am most thankful for:

Today's Date:_____

Let God speak to you through his Word. Select a scripture from Page 3.

Scripture selected:_____

Write down the scripture:

Study the scripture, then pray and answer the following.

Write down how you're feeling about the topic of the scripture:

_____

_____

_____

_____

What's your prayer to God surrounding the scripture?

_____

_____

_____

_____

Other Prayer Requests:

_____ _____
_____ _____
_____ _____
_____ _____

Answered Prayer Requests:

_____ _____
_____ _____
_____ _____
_____ _____

Today I am most thankful for:

_____
_____
_____
_____

Today's Date:_____

Let God speak to you through his Word. Select a scripture from Page 3.

Scripture selected:_____

Write down the scripture:

Study the scripture, then pray and answer the following.

~ ~ ~ ~ ~ ~

Write down how you're feeling about the topic of the scripture:

_____
_____
_____
_____

~ ~ ~ ~ ~ ~

What's your prayer to God surrounding the scripture?

_____
_____
_____
_____

Other Prayer Requests:

_____   _____
_____   _____
_____   _____
_____   _____

Answered Prayer Requests:

_____   _____
_____   _____
_____   _____
_____   _____

Today I am most thankful for:

_____
_____
_____
_____

Today's Date:_____

Let God speak to you through his Word. Select a scripture from Page 3.

Scripture selected:_____

Write down the scripture:

Study the scripture, then pray and answer the following.

Write down how you're feeling about the topic of the scripture:

_____
_____
_____
_____

What's your prayer to God surrounding the scripture?

_____
_____
_____
_____

Other Prayer Requests:

_____ _____

_____ _____

_____ _____

_____ _____

Answered Prayer Requests:

_____ _____

_____ _____

_____ _____

_____ _____

Today I am most thankful for:

_____

_____

_____

_____

Today's Date:_____

Let God speak to you through his Word. Select a scripture from Page 3.

Scripture selected:_____

Write down the scripture:

Study the scripture, then pray and answer the following.

Write down how you're feeling about the topic of the scripture:

_____

_____

_____

_____

What's your prayer to God surrounding the scripture?

_____

_____

_____

_____

Other Prayer Requests:

_____   _____
_____   _____
_____   _____
_____   _____

Answered Prayer Requests:

_____   _____
_____   _____
_____   _____
_____   _____

Today I am most thankful for:

_____
_____
_____
_____

Today's Date:_____

Let God speak to you through his Word. Select a scripture from Page 3.

Scripture selected:_____

Write down the scripture:

Study the scripture, then pray and answer the following.

Write down how you're feeling about the topic of the scripture:

_____
_____
_____
_____

What's your prayer to God surrounding the scripture?

_____
_____
_____
_____

Other Prayer Requests:

_____   _____
_____   _____
_____   _____
_____   _____

Answered Prayer Requests:

_____   _____
_____   _____
_____   _____
_____   _____

Today I am most thankful for:

_____
_____
_____
_____

Today's Date:_____

Let God speak to you through his Word. Select a scripture from Page 3.

Scripture selected:_____

Write down the scripture:

Study the scripture, then pray and answer the following.

Write down how you're feeling about the topic of the scripture:

_____

_____

_____

_____

What's your prayer to God surrounding the scripture?

_____

_____

_____

_____

Other Prayer Requests:

_____   _____
_____   _____
_____   _____
_____   _____

Answered Prayer Requests:

_____   _____
_____   _____
_____   _____
_____   _____

Today I am most thankful for:

_____
_____
_____
_____

Today's Date:_____

Let God speak to you through his Word. Select a scripture from Page 3.

Scripture selected:_____

Write down the scripture:

Study the scripture, then pray and answer the following.

Write down how you're feeling about the topic of the scripture:

_____

_____

_____

_____

What's your prayer to God surrounding the scripture?

_____

_____

_____

_____

Other Prayer Requests:

Answered Prayer Requests:

Today I am most thankful for:

Today's Date:_____

Let God speak to you through his Word. Select a scripture from Page 3.

Scripture selected:_____

Write down the scripture:

Study the scripture, then pray and answer the following.

Write down how you're feeling about the topic of the scripture:

_____
_____
_____
_____

What's your prayer to God surrounding the scripture?

_____
_____
_____
_____

Other Prayer Requests:

_____ _____

_____ _____

_____ _____

_____ _____

Answered Prayer Requests:

_____ _____

_____ _____

_____ _____

_____ _____

Today I am most thankful for:

_____

_____

_____

_____

Today's Date:_____

Let God speak to you through his Word. Select a scripture from Page 3.

Scripture selected:_____

Write down the scripture:

Study the scripture, then pray and answer the following.

Write down how you're feeling about the topic of the scripture:

_____
_____
_____
_____

What's your prayer to God surrounding the scripture?

_____
_____
_____
_____

Other Prayer Requests:

Answered Prayer Requests:

Today I am most thankful for:

Today's Date:_____

Let God speak to you through his Word. Select a scripture from Page 3.

Scripture selected:_____

Write down the scripture:

Study the scripture, then pray and answer the following.

Write down how you're feeling about the topic of the scripture:

_____

_____

_____

_____

What's your prayer to God surrounding the scripture?

_____

_____

_____

_____

Other Prayer Requests:

_____ _____
_____ _____
_____ _____
_____ _____
_____ _____

Answered Prayer Requests:

_____ _____
_____ _____
_____ _____
_____ _____
_____ _____

Today I am most thankful for:

_____
_____
_____
_____

Today's Date:_____

Let God speak to you through his Word. Select a scripture from Page 3.

Scripture selected:_____

Write down the scripture:

Study the scripture, then pray and answer the following.

Write down how you're feeling about the topic of the scripture:

_____
_____
_____
_____

What's your prayer to God surrounding the scripture?

_____
_____
_____
_____

Other Prayer Requests:

_____   _____
_____   _____
_____   _____
_____   _____

Answered Prayer Requests:

_____   _____
_____   _____
_____   _____
_____   _____

Today I am most thankful for:

_____
_____
_____
_____

Today's Date:_____

Let God speak to you through his Word. Select a scripture from Page 3.

Scripture selected:_____

Write down the scripture:

Study the scripture, then pray and answer the following.

Write down how you're feeling about the topic of the scripture:

_____

_____

_____

_____

What's your prayer to God surrounding the scripture?

_____

_____

_____

_____

Other Prayer Requests:

Answered Prayer Requests:

Today I am most thankful for:

Today's Date:_____

Let God speak to you through his Word. Select a scripture from Page 3.

Scripture selected:_____

Write down the scripture:

Study the scripture, then pray and answer the following.

Write down how you're feeling about the topic of the scripture:

_____
_____
_____
_____

What's your prayer to God surrounding the scripture?

_____
_____
_____
_____

Other Prayer Requests:

_____   _____
_____   _____
_____   _____
_____   _____

Answered Prayer Requests:

_____   _____
_____   _____
_____   _____
_____   _____

Today I am most thankful for:

_____
_____
_____
_____

Today's Date:_____

Let God speak to you through his Word. Select a scripture from Page 3.

Scripture selected:_____

Write down the scripture:

Study the scripture, then pray and answer the following.

Write down how you're feeling about the topic of the scripture:

_____

_____

_____

_____

What's your prayer to God surrounding the scripture?

_____

_____

_____

_____

Other Prayer Requests:

_____   _____
_____   _____
_____   _____
_____   _____

Answered Prayer Requests:

_____   _____
_____   _____
_____   _____
_____   _____

Today I am most thankful for:

_____
_____
_____
_____

Today's Date:_____

Let God speak to you through his Word. Select a scripture from Page 3.

Scripture selected:_____

Write down the scripture:

Study the scripture, then pray and answer the following.

Write down how you're feeling about the topic of the scripture:

_____
_____
_____
_____

What's your prayer to God surrounding the scripture?

_____
_____
_____
_____

Other Prayer Requests:

_____   _____
_____   _____
_____   _____
_____   _____

Answered Prayer Requests:

_____   _____
_____   _____
_____   _____
_____   _____

Today I am most thankful for:

_____
_____
_____
_____

Today's Date:_____

Let God speak to you through his Word. Select a scripture from Page 3.

Scripture selected:_____

Write down the scripture:

Study the scripture, then pray and answer the following.

Write down how you're feeling about the topic of the scripture:

_____

_____

_____

_____

What's your prayer to God surrounding the scripture?

_____

_____

_____

_____

Other Prayer Requests:

_____   _____
_____   _____
_____   _____
_____   _____

Answered Prayer Requests:

_____   _____
_____   _____
_____   _____
_____   _____

Today I am most thankful for:

_____
_____
_____
_____

Today's Date:_____

Let God speak to you through his Word. Select a scripture from Page 3.

Scripture selected:_____

Write down the scripture:

Study the scripture, then pray and answer the following.

Write down how you're feeling about the topic of the scripture:

_____
_____
_____
_____

What's your prayer to God surrounding the scripture?

_____
_____
_____
_____

Other Prayer Requests:

Answered Prayer Requests:

Today I am most thankful for:

Today's Date:_____

Let God speak to you through his Word. Select a scripture from Page 3.

Scripture selected:_____

Write down the scripture:

Study the scripture, then pray and answer the following.

Write down how you're feeling about the topic of the scripture:

_____
_____
_____
_____

What's your prayer to God surrounding the scripture?

_____
_____
_____
_____

Other Prayer Requests:

_____   _____
_____   _____
_____   _____
_____   _____

Answered Prayer Requests:

_____   _____
_____   _____
_____   _____
_____   _____

Today I am most thankful for:

_____
_____
_____
_____

Today's Date:_____

Let God speak to you through his Word. Select a scripture from Page 3.

Scripture selected:_____

Write down the scripture:

Study the scripture, then pray and answer the following.

Write down how you're feeling about the topic of the scripture:

_____
_____
_____
_____

What's your prayer to God surrounding the scripture?

_____
_____
_____
_____

Other Prayer Requests:

_____ _____
_____ _____
_____ _____
_____ _____

Answered Prayer Requests:

_____ _____
_____ _____
_____ _____
_____ _____

Today I am most thankful for:

_____
_____
_____
_____

Today's Date:_____

Let God speak to you through his Word. Select a scripture from Page 3.

Scripture selected:_____

Write down the scripture:

Study the scripture, then pray and answer the following.

Write down how you're feeling about the topic of the scripture:

_____

_____

_____

_____

What's your prayer to God surrounding the scripture?

_____

_____

_____

_____

Other Prayer Requests:

_____   _____
_____   _____
_____   _____
_____   _____

Answered Prayer Requests:

_____   _____
_____   _____
_____   _____
_____   _____

Today I am most thankful for:

_____
_____
_____
_____

Today's Date:_____

Let God speak to you through his Word. Select a scripture from Page 3.

Scripture selected:_____

Write down the scripture:

Study the scripture, then pray and answer the following.

Write down how you're feeling about the topic of the scripture:

_____
_____
_____
_____

What's your prayer to God surrounding the scripture?

_____
_____
_____
_____

Other Prayer Requests:

_____   _____
_____   _____
_____   _____
_____   _____

Answered Prayer Requests:

_____   _____
_____   _____
_____   _____
_____   _____

Today I am most thankful for:

_____
_____
_____
_____

Today's Date:_____

Let God speak to you through his Word. Select a scripture from Page 3.

Scripture selected:_____

Write down the scripture:

Study the scripture, then pray and answer the following.

Write down how you're feeling about the topic of the scripture:

_____

_____

_____

_____

What's your prayer to God surrounding the scripture?

_____

_____

_____

_____

Other Prayer Requests:

_____ _____
_____ _____
_____ _____
_____ _____

Answered Prayer Requests:

_____ _____
_____ _____
_____ _____
_____ _____

Today I am most thankful for:

_____
_____
_____
_____

Today's Date:_____

Let God speak to you through his Word. Select a scripture from Page 3.

Scripture selected:_____

Write down the scripture:

Study the scripture, then pray and answer the following.

Write down how you're feeling about the topic of the scripture:

_____
_____
_____
_____

What's your prayer to God surrounding the scripture?

_____
_____
_____
_____

Other Prayer Requests:

_____   _____
_____   _____
_____   _____
_____   _____

Answered Prayer Requests:

_____   _____
_____   _____
_____   _____
_____   _____

Today I am most thankful for:

_____
_____
_____
_____

Today's Date:_____

Let God speak to you through his Word. Select a scripture from Page 3.

Scripture selected:_____

Write down the scripture:

Study the scripture, then pray and answer the following.

Write down how you're feeling about the topic of the scripture:

_____
_____
_____
_____

What's your prayer to God surrounding the scripture?

_____
_____
_____
_____

Other Prayer Requests:

Answered Prayer Requests:

Today I am most thankful for:

Today's Date:_____

Let God speak to you through his Word. Select a scripture from Page 3.

Scripture selected:_____

Write down the scripture:

Study the scripture, then pray and answer the following.

Write down how you're feeling about the topic of the scripture:

_____
_____
_____
_____

What's your prayer to God surrounding the scripture?

_____
_____
_____
_____

Other Prayer Requests:

_____ _____
_____ _____
_____ _____
_____ _____

Answered Prayer Requests:

_____ _____
_____ _____
_____ _____
_____ _____

Today I am most thankful for:

_____
_____
_____
_____

Today's Date:_____

Let God speak to you through his Word. Select a scripture from Page 3.

Scripture selected:_____

Write down the scripture:

Study the scripture, then pray and answer the following.

Write down how you're feeling about the topic of the scripture:

_____
_____
_____
_____

What's your prayer to God surrounding the scripture?

_____
_____
_____
_____

Other Prayer Requests:

_____   _____
_____   _____
_____   _____
_____   _____

Answered Prayer Requests:

_____   _____
_____   _____
_____   _____
_____   _____

Today I am most thankful for:

_____
_____
_____
_____

Today's Date:_____

Let God speak to you through his Word. Select a scripture from Page 3.

Scripture selected:_____

Write down the scripture:

Study the scripture, then pray and answer the following.

Write down how you're feeling about the topic of the scripture:

_____
_____
_____
_____

What's your prayer to God surrounding the scripture?

_____
_____
_____
_____

Other Prayer Requests:

_____ _____
_____ _____
_____ _____
_____ _____

Answered Prayer Requests:

_____ _____
_____ _____
_____ _____
_____ _____

Today I am most thankful for:

_____
_____
_____
_____

Today's Date: _____

Let God speak to you through his Word. Select a scripture from Page 3.

Scripture selected: _____

Write down the scripture:

Study the scripture, then pray and answer the following.

○○○·○○○·○○○·○○○·○○○·

Write down how you're feeling about the topic of the scripture:

_____
_____
_____
_____

○○○·○○○·○○○·○○○·○○○·

What's your prayer to God surrounding the scripture?

_____
_____
_____
_____

Other Prayer Requests:

_____ _____
_____ _____
_____ _____
_____ _____

Answered Prayer Requests:

_____ _____
_____ _____
_____ _____
_____ _____

Today I am most thankful for:

_____
_____
_____
_____

Today's Date:_____

Let God speak to you through his Word. Select a scripture from Page 3.

Scripture selected:_____

Write down the scripture:

Study the scripture, then pray and answer the following.

Write down how you're feeling about the topic of the scripture:

_____
_____
_____
_____

What's your prayer to God surrounding the scripture?

_____
_____
_____
_____

Other Prayer Requests:

_____ _____
_____ _____
_____ _____
_____ _____

Answered Prayer Requests:

_____ _____
_____ _____
_____ _____
_____ _____

Today I am most thankful for:

_____
_____
_____
_____

Today's Date:_____

Let God speak to you through his Word. Select a scripture from Page 3.

Scripture selected:_____

Write down the scripture:

Study the scripture, then pray and answer the following.

Write down how you're feeling about the topic of the scripture:

_____

_____

_____

_____

What's your prayer to God surrounding the scripture?

_____

_____

_____

_____

Other Prayer Requests:

_____   _____
_____   _____
_____   _____
_____   _____

Answered Prayer Requests:

_____   _____
_____   _____
_____   _____
_____   _____

Today I am most thankful for:

_____
_____
_____
_____

Today's Date:_____

Let God speak to you through his Word. Select a scripture from Page 3.

Scripture selected:_____

Write down the scripture:

Study the scripture, then pray and answer the following.

Write down how you're feeling about the topic of the scripture:

_____
_____
_____
_____

What's your prayer to God surrounding the scripture?

_____
_____
_____
_____

Other Prayer Requests:

_____ _____
_____ _____
_____ _____
_____ _____

Answered Prayer Requests:

_____ _____
_____ _____
_____ _____
_____ _____

Today I am most thankful for:

_____
_____
_____
_____

Today's Date:_____

Let God speak to you through his Word. Select a scripture from Page 3.

Scripture selected:_____

Write down the scripture:

Study the scripture, then pray and answer the following.

Write down how you're feeling about the topic of the scripture:

_____
_____
_____
_____

What's your prayer to God surrounding the scripture?

_____
_____
_____
_____

Other Prayer Requests:

_____ _____

_____ _____

_____ _____

_____ _____

Answered Prayer Requests:

_____ _____

_____ _____

_____ _____

_____ _____

Today I am most thankful for:

_____

_____

_____

_____

Today's Date:_____

Let God speak to you through his Word. Select a scripture from Page 3.

Scripture selected:_____

Write down the scripture:

Study the scripture, then pray and answer the following.

Write down how you're feeling about the topic of the scripture:

_____
_____
_____
_____

What's your prayer to God surrounding the scripture?

_____
_____
_____
_____

Other Prayer Requests:

_____   _____
_____   _____
_____   _____
_____   _____

Answered Prayer Requests:

_____   _____
_____   _____
_____   _____
_____   _____

Today I am most thankful for:

_____
_____
_____
_____

Today's Date:_____

Let God speak to you through his Word. Select a scripture from Page 3.

Scripture selected:_____

Write down the scripture:

Study the scripture, then pray and answer the following.

Write down how you're feeling about the topic of the scripture:

_____
_____
_____
_____

What's your prayer to God surrounding the scripture?

_____
_____
_____
_____

Other Prayer Requests:

_____   _____

_____   _____

_____   _____

_____   _____

Answered Prayer Requests:

_____   _____

_____   _____

_____   _____

_____   _____

Today I am most thankful for:

_____

_____

_____

_____

Today's Date:_____

Let God speak to you through his Word. Select a scripture from Page 3.

Scripture selected:_____

Write down the scripture:

Study the scripture, then pray and answer the following.

Write down how you're feeling about the topic of the scripture:

_____
_____
_____
_____

What's your prayer to God surrounding the scripture?

_____
_____
_____
_____

Other Prayer Requests:

_____   _____
_____   _____
_____   _____
_____   _____

Answered Prayer Requests:

_____   _____
_____   _____
_____   _____
_____   _____

Today I am most thankful for:

_____
_____
_____
_____

Today's Date:_____

Let God speak to you through his Word. Select a scripture from Page 3.

Scripture selected:_____

Write down the scripture:

Study the scripture, then pray and answer the following.

Write down how you're feeling about the topic of the scripture:

_____
_____
_____
_____

What's your prayer to God surrounding the scripture?

_____
_____
_____
_____

Other Prayer Requests:

_____   _____
_____   _____
_____   _____
_____   _____

Answered Prayer Requests:

_____   _____
_____   _____
_____   _____
_____   _____

Today I am most thankful for:

_____
_____
_____
_____

Today's Date:_____

Let God speak to you through his Word. Select a scripture from Page 3.

Scripture selected:_____

Write down the scripture:

Study the scripture, then pray and answer the following.

Write down how you're feeling about the topic of the scripture:

_____
_____
_____
_____

What's your prayer to God surrounding the scripture?

_____
_____
_____
_____

Other Prayer Requests:

Answered Prayer Requests:

Today I am most thankful for:

Today's Date:_____

Let God speak to you through his Word. Select a scripture from Page 3.

Scripture selected:_____

Write down the scripture:

Study the scripture, then pray and answer the following.

Write down how you're feeling about the topic of the scripture:

_____
_____
_____
_____

What's your prayer to God surrounding the scripture?

_____
_____
_____
_____

Other Prayer Requests:

_____   _____
_____   _____
_____   _____
_____   _____

Answered Prayer Requests:

_____   _____
_____   _____
_____   _____
_____   _____

Today I am most thankful for:

_____
_____
_____
_____

Today's Date:_____

Let God speak to you through his Word. Select a scripture from Page 3.

Scripture selected:_____

Write down the scripture:

Study the scripture, then pray and answer the following.

~~~~~~~~~~

Write down how you're feeling about the topic of the scripture:

_____
_____
_____
_____

~~~~~~~~~~

What's your prayer to God surrounding the scripture?

_____
_____
_____
_____

Other Prayer Requests:

_____ _____
_____ _____
_____ _____
_____ _____

Answered Prayer Requests:

_____ _____
_____ _____
_____ _____
_____ _____

Today I am most thankful for:

_____
_____
_____
_____

Today's Date:_____

Let God speak to you through his Word. Select a scripture from Page 3.

Scripture selected:_____

Write down the scripture:

Study the scripture, then pray and answer the following.

Write down how you're feeling about the topic of the scripture:

_____

_____

_____

_____

What's your prayer to God surrounding the scripture?

_____

_____

_____

_____

Other Prayer Requests:

_____   _____
_____   _____
_____   _____
_____   _____

Answered Prayer Requests:

_____   _____
_____   _____
_____   _____
_____   _____

Today I am most thankful for:

_____
_____
_____
_____

Today's Date:_____

Let God speak to you through his Word. Select a scripture from Page 3.

Scripture selected:_____

Write down the scripture:

Study the scripture, then pray and answer the following.

Write down how you're feeling about the topic of the scripture:

_____
_____
_____
_____

What's your prayer to God surrounding the scripture?

_____
_____
_____
_____

Other Prayer Requests:

_____   _____
_____   _____
_____   _____
_____   _____

Answered Prayer Requests:

_____   _____
_____   _____
_____   _____
_____   _____

Today I am most thankful for:

_____
_____
_____
_____

Today's Date:_____

Let God speak to you through his Word. Select a scripture from Page 3.

Scripture selected:_____

Write down the scripture:

Study the scripture, then pray and answer the following.

Write down how you're feeling about the topic of the scripture:

_____
_____
_____
_____

What's your prayer to God surrounding the scripture?

_____
_____
_____
_____

Other Prayer Requests:

_____ _____
_____ _____
_____ _____
_____ _____

Answered Prayer Requests:

_____ _____
_____ _____
_____ _____
_____ _____

Today I am most thankful for:

_____
_____
_____
_____

Today's Date:_____

Let God speak to you through his Word. Select a scripture from Page 3.

Scripture selected:_____

Write down the scripture:

Study the scripture, then pray and answer the following.

Write down how you're feeling about the topic of the scripture:

_____
_____
_____
_____

What's your prayer to God surrounding the scripture?

_____
_____
_____
_____

Other Prayer Requests:

Answered Prayer Requests:

Today I am most thankful for:

Today's Date:_____

Let God speak to you through his Word. Select a scripture from Page 3.

Scripture selected:_____

Write down the scripture:

Study the scripture, then pray and answer the following.

Write down how you're feeling about the topic of the scripture:

_____
_____
_____
_____

What's your prayer to God surrounding the scripture?

_____
_____
_____
_____

Other Prayer Requests:

_____   _____

_____   _____

_____   _____

_____   _____

Answered Prayer Requests:

_____   _____

_____   _____

_____   _____

_____   _____

Today I am most thankful for:

_____

_____

_____

_____

Today's Date:_____

Let God speak to you through his Word. Select a scripture from Page 3.

Scripture selected:_____

Write down the scripture:

Study the scripture, then pray and answer the following.

Write down how you're feeling about the topic of the scripture:

_____
_____
_____
_____

What's your prayer to God surrounding the scripture?

_____
_____
_____
_____

Other Prayer Requests:

_____ _____
_____ _____
_____ _____
_____ _____

Answered Prayer Requests:

_____ _____
_____ _____
_____ _____
_____ _____

Today I am most thankful for:

_____
_____
_____
_____

Today's Date:_____

Let God speak to you through his Word. Select a scripture from Page 3.

Scripture selected:_____

Write down the scripture:

Study the scripture, then pray and answer the following.

Write down how you're feeling about the topic of the scripture:

_____

_____

_____

_____

What's your prayer to God surrounding the scripture?

_____

_____

_____

_____

Other Prayer Requests:

_____   _____
_____   _____
_____   _____
_____   _____

Answered Prayer Requests:

_____   _____
_____   _____
_____   _____
_____   _____

Today I am most thankful for:

_____
_____
_____
_____

Today's Date:_____

Let God speak to you through his Word. Select a scripture from Page 3.

Scripture selected:_____

Write down the scripture:

Study the scripture, then pray and answer the following.

Write down how you're feeling about the topic of the scripture:

_____
_____
_____
_____

What's your prayer to God surrounding the scripture?

_____
_____
_____
_____

Other Prayer Requests:

_____   _____
_____   _____
_____   _____
_____   _____
_____   _____

Answered Prayer Requests:

_____   _____
_____   _____
_____   _____
_____   _____

Today I am most thankful for:

_____
_____
_____
_____

Today's Date:_____

Let God speak to you through his Word. Select a scripture from Page 3.

Scripture selected:_____

Write down the scripture:

Study the scripture, then pray and answer the following.

Write down how you're feeling about the topic of the scripture:

_____
_____
_____
_____

What's your prayer to God surrounding the scripture?

_____
_____
_____
_____

Other Prayer Requests:

_____   _____
_____   _____
_____   _____
_____   _____

Answered Prayer Requests:

_____   _____
_____   _____
_____   _____
_____   _____

Today I am most thankful for:

_____
_____
_____
_____

Today's Date:_____

Let God speak to you through his Word. Select a scripture from Page 3.

Scripture selected:_____

Write down the scripture:

Study the scripture, then pray and answer the following.

Write down how you're feeling about the topic of the scripture:

_____

_____

_____

_____

What's your prayer to God surrounding the scripture?

_____

_____

_____

_____

Other Prayer Requests:

_____   _____
_____   _____
_____   _____
_____   _____

Answered Prayer Requests:

_____   _____
_____   _____
_____   _____
_____   _____

Today I am most thankful for:

_____
_____
_____
_____

Today's Date:_____

Let God speak to you through his Word. Select a scripture from Page 3.

Scripture selected:_____

Write down the scripture:

Study the scripture, then pray and answer the following.

Write down how you're feeling about the topic of the scripture:

_____
_____
_____
_____

What's your prayer to God surrounding the scripture?

_____
_____
_____
_____

Other Prayer Requests:

_____   _____

_____   _____

_____   _____

_____   _____

Answered Prayer Requests:

_____   _____

_____   _____

_____   _____

_____   _____

Today I am most thankful for:

_____

_____

_____

_____

Today's Date:_____

Let God speak to you through his Word. Select a scripture from Page 3.

Scripture selected:_____

Write down the scripture:

Study the scripture, then pray and answer the following.

Write down how you're feeling about the topic of the scripture:

_____
_____
_____
_____

What's your prayer to God surrounding the scripture?

_____
_____
_____
_____

Other Prayer Requests:

_____ _____

_____ _____

_____ _____

_____ _____

Answered Prayer Requests:

_____ _____

_____ _____

_____ _____

_____ _____

Today I am most thankful for:

_____

_____

_____

_____

Today's Date:_____

Let God speak to you through his Word. Select a scripture from Page 3.

Scripture selected:_____

Write down the scripture:

Study the scripture, then pray and answer the following.

Write down how you're feeling about the topic of the scripture:

_____
_____
_____
_____

What's your prayer to God surrounding the scripture?

_____
_____
_____
_____

Other Prayer Requests:

_____ _____

_____ _____

_____ _____

_____ _____

Answered Prayer Requests:

_____ _____

_____ _____

_____ _____

_____ _____

Today I am most thankful for:

_____

_____

_____

_____

Today's Date:_____

Let God speak to you through his Word. Select a scripture from Page 3.

Scripture selected:_____

Write down the scripture:

Study the scripture, then pray and answer the following.

Write down how you're feeling about the topic of the scripture:

_____
_____
_____
_____

What's your prayer to God surrounding the scripture?

_____
_____
_____
_____

Other Prayer Requests:

_____   _____
_____   _____
_____   _____
_____   _____

Answered Prayer Requests:

_____   _____
_____   _____
_____   _____
_____   _____

Today I am most thankful for:

_____
_____
_____
_____

Today's Date:_____

Let God speak to you through his Word. Select a scripture from Page 3.

Scripture selected:_____

Write down the scripture:

Study the scripture, then pray and answer the following.

Write down how you're feeling about the topic of the scripture:
_____
_____
_____
_____

What's your prayer to God surrounding the scripture?
_____
_____
_____
_____

Other Prayer Requests:

_____   _____
_____   _____
_____   _____
_____   _____

Answered Prayer Requests:

_____   _____
_____   _____
_____   _____
_____   _____

Today I am most thankful for:

_____
_____
_____
_____

Made in the USA
Las Vegas, NV
12 May 2023

71778439R00070